Mystica

MW01277195

ISBN 0 9579461 1 1 2

c 2002 Original images - Bernard Rosa

c 2002 Original text - George Helou

Concept, design, format and photography – Bernard Rosa

c 2002 Published in 2002 by Light Heart Productions Pty. Ltd.

All rights reserved. No part of this publication may be reproduced or transmitted
in any form or by any means, electronic or mechanical, including photocopying,
recording, or any information storage and retrieval system, without permission
in writing from the publisher.

Mystical Dreams is the latest book from friends Bernard Rosa and George Helou, who collaborated last year to produce the popular *Angelic Dreams*.

Bernard's vast wealth of eight years experience in Fantasy Photography has gone whole-heartedly into *Mystical Dreams*, an entirely original publication representing the conglomeration of subjects from his previous books *Fairies, Mermaids and Angelic Dreams*. He recently returned from yet another overseas tour photographing exotic locations, many of which appear in this latest work.

George meanwhile has further focused on writing the poetic thoughts, which uplift and transport you into the mystical kingdom encapsulated in every line. George's message is simple and clear, in an increasingly busy world where we forget to take time out for ourselves, stop for a short while every day to reflect, question, and be thankful for the journey on which you travel, and the places to which you may go.

Since *Angelic Dreams* was published George has moved up with the fairies to the tranquility of the Blue Mountains near Sydney, while Bernard still resides at inspirational Bondi Beach, close to the mermaids. The angels commute daily between the two.

The success of *Angelic Dreams* has enabled *Mystical Dreams* to likewise be self-published by the pair. Bernard is responsible for all visual aspects from conception of the artworks to costumes, styling and photography, through to image composition and the eventual visual layout and design of the book. Using no studios and on a limited budget, he embodies the very spirit of the message in the book; imagination and determination are his greatest resources.

All the people featured in *Mystical Dreams* are Bernard's friends and family, the only reward they seek is to be in the book. It is thanks to their generosity and also the valued assistance of Natasha, Sabina and Piers that this book has been made possible.

The words and images in *Mystical Dreams* combine in a way which allows the reader to elevate from their everyday lives and enter the magical realm within. Insightful, it is for everyone - and a positive means to help us unearth and reconnect with our ancient inner power.

Follow your dreams!

INTRODUCTION

Once upon a thought before there was time, we were involved with creating new adventures. Everything was being created as we joyfully engaged in lucid dreaming, becoming those dreams and experiencing them with no limitations. No part of these marvellous strings of adventures was feared, as the limiting ideas of pain and death were yet to be invented. Everything was possible, so nothing was mystical.

Many planetary playgrounds were formed by these extraordinary dreams, and so equipped with a body to experience it, we plunged into this heaven. Imagine observing the first appearance of dew on the first lush green leaf of a fig tree. Imagine witnessing the overwhelming arrival of the sun's first golden ray. How about the first breath-taking bloom of the smooth deeply red rose and its seductive virgin encounter with a violet blue butterfly's kiss? Your soul contains these cherished, profoundly moving memories because you were loved into all life and unconditionally afforded the privilege of observing and finally engaging all creation.

The journey evolved from a wonderful dream, driven by the innate desire to interact with what was created on Earth and far beyond. Our Spirit's instrument, the beautiful body, was blessed with the miraculous seven senses. Eyes, mouth, ears, nose, and skin are the five experiential instruments we take for granted. There are two equally wonderful senses we have made a mystery to ourselves.

The sixth sense is your psychic mind. An intuition that senses people's thoughts, perceives the future, and communicates by telepathy. Your seventh sense is even more mystical and is evidence that we were truly made in the image of God. It is the ultimate sense of knowing that you are a molecular part of everything and, at a soul and cellular level, connected to everyone.

We have arrived at a time and space where we no longer recall the divine journey that brought us here. Forgetting this journey served a meaningful and rewarding purpose. How can memory have meaning if we did not dream and experience the idea of forgetfulness? How can eternity, power and unlimited love be understood, if we never ventured into the world of ignorance or fear that allowed us to know the meaning of frustration and helplessness? For the many who have explored and become exhausted by the repetitious cycle of these emotions, the moment has ripened for the return from where we came, via the metaphysical engines of evolution.

You have a mystical potion that resides in you. This dormant elixir has the potent power for which many have searched outside themselves for thousands of years. Accessing the potion will reunite your self with all seven senses. 'Come to your senses', and engage all creation including passed away loved ones, your perfect health, colours not yet seen as well as our favourite fairies, mermaids and angels.

Nothing is unknown to the seventh sense that lays dormant in your mind, locked away by fear and doubt. Is it your time to thank this limitation for the expansion of your knowing and witness the fear dissolve as its purpose is served and solved? Knowledge and understanding will demystify that which we have dismissed as purely the imagination. What divides the imagination from reality is will and time. The separation of the impossible from possible is determined only by your personal acceptance.

Personal acceptance varies from one person to another. One person may want to believe in fairies but find it too challenging to accept their existence, while next door is a person who finds it difficult accepting anything but a world filled with magic.

Which one will experience the miracles?

George Helou

Have a light heart.

You are here
because you are loved.

Do you know why you can know fairies exist?
We exist.

Your answers are coming.

Be the pearl of life
and cloak yourself in the
eternal robe of wisdom.

Every experience
came from a dream.

7

Nature can show you
how to strip away your
superficial shell that conceals
the beautiful inner you.

How do you expect your dreams
to come true when you hold
them at a timeless distance
with the stiff arm of fear
and the stern hand of doubt?

Be clear about your dreams
and not concerned with
how they materialise.

Every person you don't forgive
estranges your ability to
love yourself.

*Embrace change
like you would a newborn child.*

14

Life is made beautiful
by attitude alone.

An open mind
is an open door to
miraculous new adventures.

*Focus on joy
and not what it takes
to be joyful.*

Your spirit soars free
through the Universe.
Why not you?

It's not what you do
but why you do it.

Truth favours the strong
and challenges the weak.

It takes more energy
to be sad
than to be joyful.

The kingdom of heaven
is within you and cannot exist
without you.

*Feed your soul
by pursuing your goals.*

*Boredom is the sign
that your soul is ready
for another exciting adventure.*

Nature's laws within you

can teach you anything

you wish to know.

Love your parents
for the gift of life.

Motherhood is the eternal
blessed child of
Mother Nature.

When you feel wonderful
because you gave,
allow the joy of giving
to be returned.

*Life is a dream
and death an illusion.
Can death be the awakening
from the illusion
we call reality?*

*Be certain
your dreams are your own
and have not been built upon
the expectations of others.*

Learn about yourself everyday
and the more you will learn
to use your great power.

The more you love,
the less you fear.

Even truth had

a beginning.

You attract those who
share your dreams.

No-one can define you.

It is not the unknown
but the fear of new adventures
that harms you.

A Mermaid's song
fills every corner of the universe
with love...
... Listen

Love and enjoy, but never worry.
No one gains from your worry.

*Innocence is your inner scent -
the divine virgin
fragrance of love.*

You belong in the moment.

Lose your fear of failure
and your failings
will lose you.

Why do you
feel the need to be accepted?

Before you can acquire wealth,

make room for it

by renouncing

your addiction to lack.

Your dreams
are as diverse and marvellous
as the starfish on the ocean bed
to the blue star
in your unlimited heaven.

Angels & Fairies

are immortal and they know

you can be too.

Without your dreams,
you have nothing.

Your intent is the essence that creates your circumstances.

Make a wish,

believe it will manifest

then forget it,

so you won't think to doubt.

Your ability to make a wish
would not exist if you did
not have the power to
make it come true.

The law of life
is clear and timeless;
you exist forever
and your home is joy.

*Wisdom is the wand
that transforms mistakes into
Evolution.*

The lotus flower can teach you things no Master can.

Is your self-doubt more powerful
than your desire
for your dreams to be realised?

*Discover what you want
to become and act it out
in every moment.
Then this is what you are.*

Make the   Universe
your   Goddess
and your journey
Eternal.

Love the freedom forever in you.

Love allows giving
without the fear of not receiving.

If you can always be yourself,

joy in all ways will be yours.

If we did not have eyes,

would the midnight stars exist?

Would we hear them instead?

You are made from an
unlimited creation & eternal joy
that is forever your identity.

Focus on your dreams

and be witness

to your magic.

Learn to grow and love.

Thoughts create your reality.
What did you create today?

When you eat food in a state of joy,
it transmutes into joyous energy.

You are Nature's eternal gift
to the Universe.

Your spirit is shared by
the Mermaid, the Angel
and the Fairy.

Align yourself with them,
and you will know
what they feel.

Seek out goodness in each person
and the divine
will ensure your reward.

The answers you receive
are only as profound
as the questions you ask.

Your most valuable resource is
Knowledge.
Your most vital tool is
Focus.

You attract what you fear
for the learning.

It's a jungle out there
when there's a jungle in you.

Love is the warming glue
that cocoons us in the
embrace of the eternal womb.

You are someone's
profound and cherished dream.

Like the fate of a flower,
your vivid petal dreams are
destined to bloom.

May the Lord of the wind
blow your sail
so you end up amongst the magic
in which you dared not believe.

Every person with whom
you have an issue is mirroring
that issue within yourself.

*Your joy patiently awaits
your uncnditional embrace.*

Build the roads
that ought to be travelled
to take you places never lived.

When you talk,
leave time for the walk.

Whatever you have thought and done,
you are unconditionally
loved and forever forgiven.

A world absent of dreams
is a world absent of life.

If you don't know
what you want
you are unable
to be fulfilled.

*Change one belief or attitude
about yourself,
and you change your
entire life.*

The truth was born from
the conception of
the first deception.

Beyond the sky are dimensions
offering realities that are
equal only to the imagination.

*Empower yourself
by respecting another's inability to
understand your point of view.*

*Only you
can empower youself
to be free.*

Choices made from emotional fear are not choices made at all.

If you are not aware of how

your opinions formed,

don't be so quick

to defend them.

The tender touch of a friend
can melt any
mountain of fear.

Love can not be built

without the

foundation of truth.

Be grateful
and full of greatness,
and you will be full of life.

Your legs and feet are just as miraculous as a mermaid's tail.

*In the face of ignorance,
manifestation masquerades
as coincidence.*

Embrace your
Grace.

You are worthy
of unconditional love.

*Love is the harmony
of a shared heartbeat.*

A Creator is your true identity.

You are in more dimensions

in any moment

than you are ever aware.

When you love yourself
you are never lonely,
even when you are alone.

Your hands and fingers
are just as wondrous as
the delicate wings of a fairy.

Every drop of water,
every ripple in the ocean
is alive with intent to nourish
your soul with new adventures.

How much time do you spend
on activities that keep you from
doing the most important things?
How seriously have you questioned
their validity?

Imagination creates knowledge.

A mystical journey begins with a leap of faith.

*You can be wise
and innocent.*

*Challenges confronted
with truth and love
make personal evolution
inevitable.*

You are the magnetic centre between past and future.

Be patient and realise
you have all the time in the
Universe to create miracles.

Give for love, forgive with love.

Risk new adventures and trust the Universe will reward your efforts to evolve your soul.

The mystical merge
of love into life is the
Divine chemistry
of all creation.

Dance is the sacred ritual
that lets the body interpret the
sublime language of sound.

Listen to Nature's symphony.
It can transport you to places
you've never been.

Maintaining your focus
on this world will keep you
away from other worlds.

*The challenge of truthfulness
evokes more fear than
the ease of sowing lies.*

*Even asleep, you are observed
with love.*

159

*Be indefinable by race, colour or creed
and you are inseparable from
the mind of God.*

Being unaware of your thoughts

is like drifting without oars

down the river of life.

You are the creator of your habits,
and the master of their undoing.

Know yourself to
know you can.

The mistake most worth avoiding
is the one you've made before.

Where would you be and what would you do,
if all your dreams came true?

Special thanks to:-

Our parents, Natasha, Sabina,

Janine, Georgia, Piers,

Ramtha, Fuji Film.

Make-up:

Larissa Kogan

Andrea Szasz

www.bernardrosa.com

You are divine and your thoughts create reality.